JUL   1993

KN

The
John
Adamses

by
Cass R. Sandak

CRESTWOOD HOUSE
New York

Maxwell Macmillan Canada
Toronto

Maxwell Macmillan International
New York Oxford Singapore Sydney

Library of Congress Cataloging-in-Publication Data
Sandak, Cass R.
    The John Adamses / by Cass R. Sandak. — 1st ed.
        p. cm. — (First families)
    Includes bibliographical references and index.
    Summary: Examines the life of the second American president and his family, from his childhood to his final
days in Massachusetts.
    ISBN 0-89686-640-8
    1. Adams, John, 1735–1826—Juvenile literature. 2. Adams family—Juvenile literature. 3. Presidents—United
States—Biography—Juvenile literature. [1. Adams, John, 1735–1826. 2. Adams, Abigail, 1744–1818. 3. Presidents.
4. First ladies.] I. Title. II. Series: Sandak, Cass R. First families.
[E322.S24   1992]
973.4′092—dc20
[B]   92-9262

Macmillan Publishing Company   Maxwell Macmillan Canada, Inc.
866 Third Avenue   1200 Eglinton Avenue East
New York, NY 10022   Suite 200
                                      Don Mills, Ontario M3C 3N1

CRESTWOOD HOUSE

Macmillan Publishing Company is part of the Maxwell Communication Group of Companies.

Produced by Flying Fish Studio

Printed in the United States of America

First edition

10 9 8 7 6 5 4 3 2 1

Contents

The White House was not yet finished when John Adams and his family moved in.

The Brand-new White House

On November 1, 1800, John Adams moved into the newly built White House. Adams and his wife, Abigail, were the first presidential family to live there. Adams had only four months of his term left to serve. Washington, D.C., was a new city that had been built on the banks of the Potomac River. It was to be the nation's capital.

The house was not yet finished. Abigail was still at the Adamses' home in Massachusetts attending to family business. It would be two more weeks before she could join her husband. The house was certainly larger and grander than the Adamses were accustomed to, although in France they had lived in a lovely palace set amid formal gardens.

When President Adams moved in, the White House was not the building we know today. Only six rooms were remotely habitable. Most of the surrounding land was a huge mud hole. Builders' tools were strewn around makeshift construction shacks. Inside, the building was damp and cold. The plasterwork had not dried completely.

When Abigail Adams joined her husband, she found much to dislike. There wasn't a suitable backyard for hanging her laundry, so she instructed her servants to hang clothing to dry in the grand spaces of the East Room. Like many of the other rooms, the East Room did not yet have plaster on its walls.

Mrs. Adams was also annoyed that there were no bells with which to summon the servants. More importantly, there was no indoor plumbing. The family had to walk to a privy in the backyard. Water had to be carried from an outdoor pump that was nearly half a mile away.

The Adamses could not even obtain firewood to warm the house. Servants were in short supply and no one was available to provide fuel.

Mrs. Adams wrote to her daughter, "There is not a single apartment finished." One of Mrs. Adams's first jobs was to find a spot for one of the earliest White House treasures. She had to hang Gilbert Stuart's portrait of George Washington. Completed in 1797, the painting has been prominently displayed in the East Room ever since. Washington was the country's first president. John Adams was its second.

Adams wrote in a letter to his wife the invocation that is now carved into the marble in the State Dining Room mantelpiece: "I pray heaven to bestow the best of blessings on this house and on all that shall hereafter inhabit it. May none but honest and wise men ever rule under this roof."

John Adams's birthplace

Young John Adams

John Adams was born October 30, 1735, in the town of Braintree, Massachusetts. In 1792 the name of Braintree was changed to Quincy. Some sources give Adams's birthdate as October 19 (Old Style). This is due to a difference in calendars. For many years, the Old Style calendar was still used both in England and in the English colonies. It was not until 1752 that the New Style calendar was adopted in these places.

John Adams's father was a church elder, or deacon, also named John Adams. Young John had two brothers, Peter and Elihu, both of whom were born after John. The senior Adams was a farmer in Braintree. He was descended from the Puritans who had set up the Massachusetts Bay Colony in the 1600s. The family kept strict religious traditions.

The Adamses were socially prominent and reasonably well off. Deacon Adams was respected as shrewd, intelligent and practical. John's mother was Susanna Boylston Adams. She came from a wealthy family. Many people thought that by marrying Susanna Boylston, the senior John Adams was stepping above his station. Both mother and son were said to be talkative—and bright.

The house where John Adams was born was a typical New England saltbox house with clapboard siding. There were four large rooms on two floors. These included a sitting room and kitchen downstairs and two bedrooms upstairs.

Young John was bright and enjoyed his lessons. Deacon Adams planned a career in the church for his son John. When John was growing up, he spent long hours in church listening to fiery sermons. And John also spent a great deal of his free time discussing religious questions concerning the nature of God and His part in human affairs.

When Adams was young he developed a love of debate and argument. This led him away from the church and into a career in law. Young John started to get lazy in his subjects, and he needed special tutoring in order to get into college.

Schoo̅l

Adams at Harvard

First(John Adams was a teenager—just 16—when he enrolled at Harvard University in Cambridge, Massachusetts. Situated near Boston, Harvard was the first college set up in the English colonies. The school already had more than 100 years of tradition behind it when John Adams went there.)

Harvard University at the time Adams studied there

John's father had to sell 30 acres of his precious farm-land in order to raise the money for John's education. During his days at Harvard, Adams reconsidered whether he wanted to be a minister. In the end, the church lost out. Still, Adams wasn't sure what he wanted to do with his life. When he graduated from Harvard, he moved to Worcester, Massachusetts, and taught school for one year. Then Adams became homesick. And he was beginning to think that he would like to practice law.

Adams became a lawyer three years after he graduated from Harvard. First he practiced in Braintree. Then, as he frequently needed to make the ten-mile trip to Boston, he set up a law practice there. During his years living in the city, Adams changed his residences at least three times.

As an adult, Adams was short and stocky. He was five feet seven inches tall and was always self-conscious about his stoutness. As he grew older he began to put on more weight.

John Adams's father died of influenza in 1761. Adams inherited the family farm. It was called Penn's Hill Farm. The homestead included two houses that were almost identical, a barn and about 40 acres of land. All he needed was a wife and family to make his life complete. Then he met Abigail Smith.

John Adams became a successful lawyer in the colonies.

Abigail Smith

Abigail Smith was born on November 11, 1744, in Weymouth, in the Massachusetts colony. Her parents were William Smith and Elizabeth Quincy Smith. The family had been prominent in public life for several generations. Smith was a clergyman from Weymouth. He had also gone to Harvard, and had graduated in 1725. For 50 years Abigail's father served as minister of Weymouth's First, or North, Parish. Her grandfather had spent 21 years in the Massachusetts House of Representatives. He was also on the supreme court of the colony.

As a young girl Abigail was often sick. Because of this she was unable to have any formal schooling, even though she grew up in an intellectual household. Abigail would later resent that she had not received the same schooling as her brothers. Her father tutored her in many subjects and saw that she was given ample opportunity to use her mind. She also learned a great deal from her grandfather Quincy. Both men had libraries of several thousand volumes. Abigail was instructed in mathematics, philosophy, Latin and Greek as well as economics.

Abigail was clearheaded, strong-minded and practical. She was also a keen observer and a thoughtful writer.

Although John and Abigail had met before, they did not know each other well. But they soon became close. Abigail's mother thought briefly of opposing her daughter's marriage. But Abigail was a strong willed and independent woman, so her mother soon gave in to her daughter's wishes.

Abigail came from a well-educated, prominent family.

The Adams Family

On October 25, 1764, Adams married Abigail Smith. She was not yet 20 when her father joined the couple in matrimony. Often Adams's work took him away from his wife and family during their marriage. So they wrote letters to each other while they were apart. These letters are moving documents of a very happy marriage—and of the times in which it took place.

After their marriage the couple lived on their nine-acre farm in Braintree. John Adams was a successful lawyer, and Abigail began to raise the couple's children. Their firstborn was a daughter named Abigail Amelia, called Nabby by most of the family. The rest of the Adams children included three boys: John Quincy, Charles and Thomas Boylston. The couple also had another daughter, Susanna, who died in infancy.

By all accounts the Adamses were demanding parents with high standards. They were affectionate, but they did not always approve of the younger generation's behavior and opinions. On the subject of child rearing, Abigail wrote, "[Do] not teach what to think, but how to think and they will learn how to act."

With Abigail's early training in mathematics and economics, it was only natural that John Adams turn over many responsibilities to her. She managed the family farm. John also left finances and investments in his wife's capable hands. An astute businesswoman, Abigail continued to make money in rising and falling markets well into her sixties.

Often John's work as a lawyer took him to Boston, and he would be away from home for long periods. His family wanted to see what life in a big city was like, so in the spring of 1768 the Adamses moved to Boston.

In Boston they realized how isolated they had been on their farm. They had, of course, known about the 1765 Stamp Act. This law forced the colonists to pay the British government to put stamps on documents to make them legal. This was just one of many insults from Great Britain.

Many of the colonists in Boston refused to buy or use goods that had been shipped from England. The Adamses joined in the boycott and did not serve tea. And they wore clothing that had been made in the colonies rather than imported from abroad.

John Adams's law office

Trouble in Boston

Then in March 1770 came the so-called Boston Massacre. British officers were trying to maintain order among the colonists. They fired their guns into a seething, rock-throwing mob of Boston citizens who had become enraged over Britain's treatment of the colonists. Five citizens were killed and many were wounded.

John Adams undertook the defense of the British soldiers who were on trial for murder. When the trial was over, he was able to secure the acquittal of all but two of the soldiers. Even though the acquittal went against his anti-British feelings, Adams was an honest man. He thought that everyone had the right to a fair trial.

A print showing the Boston Massacre

The Boston Tea Party, when colonists dumped 300 chests of tea into the harbor as an act of protest against unjust taxes

The reaction of Boston's citizens was mixed. Most believed that the colonists had been right in protesting. But they also believed in law and order and thought that the officers had only been performing their duty.

As a result of his legal work in defending the soldiers involved in the Boston Massacre, Adams skyrocketed to fame. The people of Boston elected him to the Massachusetts colonial legislature.

Then in 1773 came the final insult to Bostonians. In December three shiploads of tea arrived from overseas. Local protesters dressed up as Indians and went down to the harbor. There they boarded the ships and dumped the cargo—300 chests of tea—overboard. The event became known as the Boston Tea Party. Great Britain closed the port and effectively shut Boston off from all imported goods.

Life during the War

In June 1774 the Adamses left Boston. They had had enough of life in the big city during dangerous times. They moved back to their Braintree farm. Shortly thereafter, John Adams journeyed to Philadelphia, Pennsylvania. There he served as one of four delegates from Massachusetts to the Continental Congress. The delegates' job was to make a list of grievances against the king of England. Perhaps the list could be turned into a declaration of some kind. Adams impressed the other delegates as having "the clearest head and firmest heart of any man in Congress."

Adams emerged as a leader in the drive for independence. In fact, he became such a vehement supporter of a break with England that he was regarded as an extremist and people were almost afraid of him. As bright and persuasive as he was, to many people Adams remained an unpopular figure.

Work in the Continental Congress kept Adams in Philadelphia for long periods of time. But he was sometimes able to return home to his family. And war with England was drawing closer. In 1775 fighting began not far from Boston—first at Lexington and then at Concord.

All during this long stretch, Abigail stayed at home with their children. The letters exchanged between John and Abigail Adams tell us much about the revolutionary war period. They provide insights into the effects of the war on the lives of the people living through this turbulent time.

Back in Philadelphia, the Continental Congress met once more to finish its work. Public opinion became more

The signing of the Declaration of Independence

and more vocal in favor of separating from England. A document was needed to set forth the reasons the colonists wanted independence. John Adams was one of five men chosen to help write the Declaration of Independence. All through the hot June days of 1776 the drafters worked on getting the language just right. Finally on July 2 the document was signed. It was made public on July 4.

Time Abroad

After the Declaration of Independence was signed in Philadelphia, John Adams hoped to return home to Abigail and their family. He wanted to pursue his law practice and tend his farm. But fate held different orders for him.

Because of Adams's strong diplomatic skills he was sent to Europe to negotiate a peace treaty with the French. John and his son John Quincy left in 1778 for France. Abigail stayed at home.

John Quincy Adams accompanied his father to Europe as the elder Adams sought to win support from the French during the revolutionary war.

After an Atlantic crossing that lasted two months, father and son finally arrived in France. Their voyage had been plagued both by storms and by enemy vessels.

While he was in France, Adams confided state secrets to Abigail in his letters. He forwarded his own notes and diaries to her for safekeeping. Under no conditions could she reveal the contents to anyone.

When the American Revolution began, France was still a monarchy. Yet the country provided some of the firmest backing for the colonists. Without French help, the colonies' bid to sever their ties with England might have been less successful. Philosophically, the concept of freedom appealed to the French. And they were also interested in opposing their longtime rival, Great Britain.

And yet now that the United States was established, the French refused to recognize the new country. Adams thought the problem was hopeless, and asked to return to the United States. He came back for a three-month period in 1780. But Congress sent him right back to Europe.

This time Adams was also sent to Holland to seek a loan from the Dutch government to keep the United States afloat. Adams was able to do this with little difficulty. Then, just as Adams's frustrations with France reached their peak, a breakthrough came. In 1781 the final battles of the American Revolution were fought. Finally in 1783 the French officially recognized the new country. Peace was at hand, and Adams, who was instrumental in the peace negotiations, shuttled between London and Paris. In 1783 the Treaty of Paris formally ended the war.

Letters sustained Abigail and John during the long periods when they were apart.

A Life in Letters

During one four-and-a-half-year period, the Adamses did not once see each other. This separation proved to be almost more than Abigail could bear. Cruel gossip suggested that Adams was staying away from Abigail because the two had marital problems. In despair, Abigail wrote to her husband in London assuring him that her solitude was soothed by her faith in his loyalty: "[I have] unbounded confidence . . . in your attachment to me." However, she went on to complain, "[This] cruel world too often injures my feelings by wondering how a person possessed of domestic attachments can sacrifice them by absenting himself for years."

22

Adams was touched by his wife's letter and soon wrote back asking her to join him. By 1783 Abigail had sailed for England to be reunited with her husband. She brought along their daughter Nabby, now 18, and joined her husband and John Quincy, who had turned 16. The Adamses now spent another four-year period living abroad. The refinement and stimulation of European life greatly appealed to them.

While in Paris in 1784, the Adamses lived in an elegant and spacious mansion surrounded by formal gardens. They were entranced by Paris and the French. "If you ask me what is the business of life in France, I answer pleasure," Abigail wrote.

The Adamses lived first in France for eight months. They then moved to London, where Adams was named the first American minister to Great Britain. The Adamses lived in London for nearly four years.

The time spent in England was fateful for the whole family. While the Adamses were in London, William Stephens Smith, a former American officer during the revolutionary war, became Adams's secretary. He met the Adamses' daughter Nabby, fell in love and married her.

William Stephens Smith, Adams's secretary in England, fell in love with Adams's daughter, Nabby.

23

Louisa Catherine Johnson, future wife of John Quincy Adams

At the same time, John Quincy Adams met his future wife. He was just 17 years old. The lady was Louisa Catherine Johnson. She was the English-born daughter of an American merchant, Thomas Johnson.

The Adamses were well received in London by King George III and Queen Charlotte. They adapted quickly to court life. One rumor even had it that John Quincy Adams was set to marry one of the royal princesses until George Washington intervened with Adams to discourage the match. Some American critics even took to equating John Quincy Adams with the Prince of Wales. They feared the beginning of a new royalist alliance that would once more make Americans subjects of a king.

The Adamses returned from Europe in 1788 determined to live a quiet and refined life as farmers at Borland Place. This was a farm that Adams had purchased through a friend while he was still living in England. The Adamses had remembered it as one of the most elegant homes in Braintree. But having spent so much time abroad, they found the house cramped and rustic compared to the grand houses and palaces of Europe. It would be several years before Peacefield, as they renamed the house, would be expanded and remodeled to suit the Adamses' needs and tastes.

Peacefield in the late 1700s

The Vice President

John Adams had been out of the country for nearly ten years. A lot had happened during that time. The Constitution had been written. One of the nation's first tasks was to find people to lead the new country. According to the Constitution, the two people who received the largest number of electoral votes would become president and vice president. In 1789 George Washington won the greatest number of votes and John Adams the second largest. This made Washington president and John Adams vice president.

Adams was the sort of person who wasn't happy being in second place. He thought that his statesmanship should have made him president. After all, Washington had almost no experience except as a military leader. Serving as vice president was not an entirely satisfactory experience for Adams. The office did not provide much in the way of stimulation or responsibility. To his wife he said, "My country has in its wisdom contrived for me the most insignificant office that ever the invention of man contrived or his imagination conceived."

During Washington's presidency, the capital of the country was New York City. While he was vice president, Adams lived in a mansion in Richmond Hill. It was situated in a suburb north of the settled lower portion of Manhattan Island.

It would have been fascinating to witness Abigail Adams's first meeting with the first lady, Martha Washington. Abigail Adams was a feisty New Englander and Martha Washington was an aristocratic southerner. Abigail

Martha Washington formed a close friendship with Abigail Adams.

was an intellectual who was probably sterner than Martha. Martha had been brought up in the gracious tradition of plantation hospitality.

Actually, Abigail Adams greatly admired Martha Washington. She found the first lady's character "modest and unassuming, dignified and feminine." Mrs. Adams also thought that Mrs. Washington was more attractive than she was. Writing of her relationship with Martha, Abigail confided, "We live upon terms of much friendship." Indeed, the two women had even spent a three-day holiday together in New Jersey.

America's first political parties developed while George Washington was still president. Adams and Alexander Hamilton were recognized as leaders of the Federalists, who supported a strong central government for the country. The other party, which included Thomas Jefferson, was called the Democratic-Republican party. It stood for strong states' rights with a weaker federal government. Oddly, Jefferson would end up being Adams's vice president although the two had opposing political viewpoints.

It was during Adams's first term as vice president that his Federalist point of view was seen most clearly. Washington and Adams were reelected and served a second term, from 1793 to 1797. During this period, the seat of government moved from New York City to Philadelphia. Philadelphia remained the nation's capital until the move to Washington, D.C., in 1800.

A Happy Family

Abigail managed the Adams household and farms. She also controlled family finances and raised the couple's four children, preparing them for active, useful lives.

John Quincy was the most successful of the children, although his mother never fully approved of his choice of an English wife. He served in a number of important positions. At 14 he was secretary to the minister to Russia.

John Quincy Adams also served as U.S. ambassador to England in 1815. He held several distinguished government positions, including secretary of state, before he became the sixth president of the United States in 1825.

Both Thomas and Charles Adams were heavy drinkers and died very young.

The letters that John and Abigail wrote to each other are filled with intelligent observation, insight and a keen sense of humor. The Adamses remained deeply in love and devoted to each other. Both were plain and practical. They were also opinionated and frank, stubborn and ready to defend their views.

After 50 years of marriage, Abigail could still write to her sister: "My first choice would be the same if I again had youth and opportunity to make it."

Feminists have claimed Abigail as a very progressive woman for her time. She was a very modern woman and well read in the political philosophy of her period. She thought that women should have rights equal to men and should be allowed to vote. Abigail Adams was against slavery. She also believed in education for both sexes.

When her husband was involved in drafting the Declaration of Independence, she said, "I desire you would remember the ladies and be more generous and favorable to them than your ancestors. Do not put such unlimited power in the hands of husbands." Abigail wrote, "Remember all men would be tyrants if they could."

President John Adams

John Adams served the office of vice president well even though he felt it was not a fitting position for himself. He supported George Washington as the country's choice for president. So it is not surprising that Adams was a leading candidate to become president in the election of 1796. Adams was the Federalist candidate, while Thomas Jefferson was the Democratic-Republican choice. When the votes were tallied, Adams came in first and Jefferson second. Thus Jefferson, Adams's opponent, became Adams's vice president.

Adams became the nation's second president in 1797. He was 61 years old when he took the oath of office in Philadelphia on March 4. Abigail was not by his side, as she was taking care of Adams's sick mother back in Massachusetts.

Adams tended to be viewed as an elitist. He was charged with trying to restrict power to a select body of men. He usually gave people jobs based on their ability without regard to their party standing. But sometimes, with Abigail's backing, he gave positions to relatives, not based strictly on their abilities. He spent much of his time in Massachusetts and not in the center of activity in Washington.

The Adams presidency was a stormy period. In the early summer of 1798 the Alien and Sedition acts were signed. These laws were designed to help protect the government

John Adams was 61 years old when he became the second president of the United States.

31

of the new country from harmful influences. Adams and his wife feared an influx of foreigners into the country. They were afraid of plots against the government and even of assassination attempts against themselves.

George Washington died at Mount Vernon in December 1799. Although the Adamses and Washingtons were good friends, John and Abigail Adams were not able to attend the funeral. The trip from Philadelphia to Virginia would have taken several days, and they could not get there in time for the funeral.

That same December John Adams delivered the first State of the Union Address. Abigail did not think it proper for her to attend, but she did not discourage their daughter Nabby from going to hear her father speak.)

The XYZ Affair

Relations with France came back to haunt Adams during his time in office. France was still a powerful seafaring nation. French sailors tried to seize American ships. Some people even talked of the possibility of war.

President Adams sent an envoy of three representatives to France. But Talleyrand, the French foreign minister, and the other members of the government refused to meet with them. At this time the government of France in the postrevolutionary period was known as the Directory. These people said they would acknowledge the new American government only if the United States would pay them a huge sum of money. In effect, the money would amount to a bribe.

A cartoon of the day shows the United States resisting the threats and demands for money from France, depicted as a monster.

When Adams learned of the incident in the spring of 1798 he reported it to Congress. The Senate printed the president's statement. But the statement identified the three leaders of the Directory only as X, Y and Z. Hence the event became known as the XYZ Affair.

The event prompted an American envoy to utter the rallying cry: "Millions for defense, but not one cent for tribute." The United States refused payment, and finally the French gave in. By 1800 cordial relations with France had been restored.

The First Lady in Philadelphia

Abigail was undoubtedly a strong influence on her husband. Mrs. Adams did not always see eye to eye with the president, but she was wise enough to hold her tongue. When relations with France were at their worst, Mrs. Adams was all for going to war with the country. Fortunately, the president kept a cool head. Although they agreed on many issues, Abigail frequently found she had to subordinate her opinions to those of her husband.

Abigail was regarded by the public as not quite fashionable and slightly prudish. Many people thought Abigail Adams was too strong a personality and had too much political influence over her husband. She was dubbed Her Majesty and Madame President by some.

As first lady in Philadelphia, Mrs. Adams rose at 5:00 A.M. The earliest hours were devoted to correspondence and domestic affairs. These included menu planning and giving orders to the household staff. In the afternoons, Mrs. Adams returned social calls or met with people who came to see her.

On Tuesday and Thursday evenings, Mrs. Adams opened her drawing room for "salons," in the French fashion. Friends and influential people in the worlds of politics and the arts would gather for lively conversation and sometimes for musical entertainment. Every other evening Abigail and her husband had dinner together. Sometimes there were friends or other family members present.

Abigail was always careful with family finances. She found that, as public figures, she and John often had to entertain prominent officials and political figures at their own expense. She resented this and found that it sometimes left the family short of cash for immediate needs, such as paying their tax bill.

Often during the presidency Mrs. Adams was not in Philadelphia. She remained at their family home in Quincy. Running the farm and looking after other family business absorbed much of her time. She was now in her mid-fifties and ill health sometimes plagued her. On one occasion yellow fever nearly claimed her life.

A Home for the Nation

The Adamses entertained in the new capitol much as they had in Philadelphia. The Adamses and the Washingtons before them expected people to pay total respect to them. And since all they knew was European, there was a great deal of bowing and scraping.

Once a week the president and his wife held receptions. These were known as levées. During these receptions, the Adamses greeted many important people. But the atmosphere was always stiff, formal and European. The Adamses, after all, liked French things, so it is not surprising that they would pattern the entertainment at the White House after the French. And this set the tone for entertaining in Washington.

Even though the White House was far from elegant

when they moved in, the Adamses soon made it livable. Visitors to the house were astonished by the elegance of the dwelling and its well-proportioned rooms. The interior walls were white and the draperies were white with gold fringe. Much of the furniture was covered in rich red damask.

The Adamses celebrated the first Christmas in the White House. In 1800 they hosted the first holiday parties. Children were active and joined in the fun. The Adamses' son Charles had one daughter named Susanna. She was orphaned early, after her father died of alcoholism. As a four-year-old she came to the White House to live with her grandparents. She was the first child to live at the White House. That Christmas she was given a set of china dishes for her doll, but a jealous playmate smashed them at the Christmas party. President Adams himself had to step in to soothe the unhappy child.

Because the building was unfinished, it was drafty and cold. Susanna was often sick with whooping cough, which may have been aggravated by the dampness of the building. Certainly the damp chill made her grandmother's rheumatism more acute. Although much of the area surrounding the White House was dense forest, it was almost impossible to find servants to chop enough wood to keep fires burning in the White House fireplaces. Finally, after she had been living in the uncomfortable house for two weeks, Mrs. Adams went to Congress to lobby for help. Congress agreed, and shortly after that the Adamses hired a handyman to take care of some of the odd jobs around the house.

Abigail Adams in old age

During Christmas of 1800 Mrs. Adams burned large amounts of wood in the White House fireplaces, just to make the place cheery and to keep it warm. The Adamses even called their Christmas dinner "A Most Sinful Feast." As well as turkey they served roast ham and a great roast beef. To finish off the celebration, there were eight different desserts, including mince pie and rich plum pudding.

The Adamses gave the first White House New Year's Day reception on January 1, 1801. It was held in what is now called the oval Yellow Room. But it was still unfinished at that time.

A Second Term?

In the early days of the United States, members of the president's cabinet would remain even when the next president came into office. It had not occurred to anyone that a person who had served George Washington well would not necessarily work well with John Adams in office. Alexander Hamilton was such a person. Even though he had served as Washington's chief adviser, he was no friend of John Adams. In fact, Hamilton did not think highly of Adams. He also had a great deal to do with the poor state of poor relations with France.

Alexander Hamilton did not think highly of Adams and managed to make sure that Thomas Jefferson would be president instead.

It was Hamilton who caused Adams to lose a second term as president. A skilled backstage manipulator, Hamilton managed to spread gossip about Adams. As a result, Thomas Jefferson became the nation's third president. In the election of November 1800, Adams garnered only a few less electoral votes than Thomas Jefferson did— 65 to Jefferson's 73. But those few votes cost Adams the presidency, because Aaron Burr of New York also won 73 votes. (To decide the tie between the two Democratic-Republicans, the House of Representatives voted again in February 1801, making Jefferson president and Burr vice president on the 36th ballot.)

After the White House

When Jefferson was inaugurated as president, Adams resented having to turn over the reins of government to him. In fact, he left Washington before the inauguration.

Adams's retirement was spent on the family farm in Quincy, Massachusetts. This was the farm he had bought when he and Mrs. Adams returned from Europe in 1788. The Adamses had added some rooms and named it Peacefield after the peace he had negotiated with France. It was a small but comfortable home for the couple. His beloved Abigail died in 1818, but Adams lived eight more years.

Peacefield, as it looks today

John Adams and Thomas Jefferson had earlier been close friends. But their split on political issues had caused a break in the friendship. In old age, Adams was able to repair some of the damage, and the two men corresponded once more.

On July 4, 1826, family members asked Adams if knew what day it was. His response showed that his keen mind was still sharp. "Oh yes. It is the glorious Fourth of July. God bless it!" But he then lapsed into a coma. On his deathbed that same day Adams's last hoarse whisper was "Thomas Jefferson still survives." As it turned out, Jefferson had died only a few hours earlier at his Virginia estate, Monticello. Adams was 90 when he died, propped up in a wing chair in the corner of his study.

Both Abigail and John Adams were buried in the crypt of the United First Parish Church on Hancock Street in Quincy, Massachusetts. Many years later, when their son John Quincy Adams and his wife died, they too were buried in the same place.

The Adams Legacy

As the second president, Adams was more a creator than an inheritor of tradition. He was thoughtful and well educated. He was a better philosopher than politician.

He was one of the earliest supporters of the patriots' cause. He was sent as a delegate to the first and second

Continental congresses. On both occasions he served on more than 90 key committees. He spearheaded the drive for independence.

Unlike Washington, he was not a military personality. He had spent most of the war years in France and Holland. During this period he served as a diplomat for the emerging country. He was able to secure military and financial help for the United States. He also helped negotiate the peace treaty that ended the American Revolution.

Of the Founding Fathers, John Adams probably had one of the finest minds. He was the best educated and probably the most cultivated of all the leaders. Thomas Jefferson may have had broader interests and more startling achievements, but John Adams probably had the most highly developed political philosophy.

Since President Adams's time, the Adams family has been prominent in American politics and literature. His son, John Quincy Adams, became president. His grandson was a minister to Great Britain. And his great-grandson, Henry Adams, was a famous historian and writer.

Many years afterward, Charles Francis Adams, John Quincy Adams's son and John Adams's grandson, inherited the Peacefield property. On the grounds of the property he built a 19th-century stone building to house a library containing the books and papers of the distinguished family. He spent more than four decades cataloging and arranging the collection for use by scholars.

Conclusion

Many people feel that it was John Adams who was able to get the Declaration of Independence accepted and signed. And we know that John Adams was the person who decided that the Fourth of July should be celebrated as the great day of independence. It seems most fitting that Adams died on the Fourth of July—exactly 50 years after the first Independence Day.

The United First Parish Church in Quincy, Massachusetts, where both John and Abigail Adams are buried

For Further Reading

Anthony, Carl Sferrazza. *First Ladies: The Saga of the Presidents' Wives and Their Power, 1789–1961.* New York: William Morrow and Company, Inc., 1990.

Brill, Marlene Targ. *Encyclopedia of the Presidents: John Adams.* Chicago: Childrens Press, 1986.

Fisher, Leonard Everett. *The White House.* New York: Holiday House, 1989.

Friedel, Frank. *The Presidents of the United States of America.* Revised edition. Washington, D.C.: The White House Historical Association, 1989.

Klapthor, Margaret Brown. *The First Ladies.* Revised edition. Washington, D.C.: The White House Historical Association, 1989.

Levin, Phyllis Lee. *Abigail Adams.* New York: St. Martin's Press, 1987.

Lindsay, Rae. *The Presidents' First Ladies.* New York: Franklin Watts, 1989.

The Living White House. Revised edition. Washington, D.C.: The White House Historical Association, 1987.

Osborne, Angela. *Abigail Adams.* New York: Chelsea House, 1989.

St. George, Judith. *The White House: Cornerstone of a Nation.* New York: G. P. Putnam's Sons, 1990.

Stefoff, Rebecca. *John Adams, 2nd President of the United States.* Ada, Okla.: Garrett Educational Corporation, 1988.

Index